Contents

SO-AZI-552

To D.F.B. and T.R.B. with love

Special thanks to Toni Vinyl

Kermy and Pepper

by Leslie Ellen
Illustrated by Dara Goldman

Modern Curriculum Press

Modern Curriculum Press

An Imprint of Pearson Learning
299 Jefferson Road, P.O. Box 480
Parsippany, NJ 07054–0480

http://www.mcschool.com

Credits
Illustrations: Dara Goldman

Computer colorizations: Lucie Maragni

Cover and book design by Lisa Ann Arcuri

ISBN: 0–7652–1360-5

1 2 3 4 5 6 7 8 9 10 LB 08 07 06 05 04 03 02 01 00 99

1 · Pepper and Tabby

"Good-bye, Pepper," said Max as he put on his backpack. "I'll see you when I get home from school."

Max waved good-bye to his dad and walked quickly to the school bus.

After Max left the house, Pepper jumped up. She looked through the window and watched. Max climbed onto the school bus. The door of the bus closed, and Max was gone.

"Don't worry, Pepper," said Dad. "Max will be home before you know it."

After Dad left for work, Pepper was glum. She had no one to play with until Max came home.

Tabby, the cat, was home. Tabby was very big. Tabby was also very old and a little bit grumpy.

Tabby sometimes growled at Pepper. Pepper wanted to play. Tabby did not.

The time passed slowly. Pepper waited and waited for Max to come home. Max was late.

Soon Pepper heard sounds outside. Max and his mom were coming.

The door opened. In came Max and his mom. Max was carrying a box. The box had small holes all over it. Max's mom was carrying a large cage.

Max opened the box very carefully. Out stepped a bird. The bird was green and white. He had shiny black eyes and an orange beak.

Max looked over at Tabby. Tabby was fast asleep. Then Max petted Pepper and pointed to the bird.

"Pepper," said Max, "this is Kermy. Kermy is a parrot. Some of the feathers on Kermy's wings have been trimmed. He doesn't fly very well," Max told Pepper.

Kermy was spinning in circles on the floor. Max and his mom started laughing.

"Mom," asked Max, "when will Kermy start to talk?"

"The vet said that Kermy is old enough to begin talking now," said Mom. "We'll have to train him."

Pepper looked at Max. She looked at Mom. Then she looked at Kermy.

Chapter 3 · Friends

As the days went by, Max tried to teach Kermy to talk. Over and over Max said, "Hello, hello!"

Kermy looked at Max. He looked at Pepper when Pepper barked her hello. But Kermy did not talk.

Kermy had a large cage where his food and water were kept. The door of Kermy's cage was always open. Kermy hopped out whenever he wanted.

Kermy had lots of toys. One of his favorite toys was a small ball with a bell inside. Kermy liked to roll the ball with his beak.

One morning after Max left for school,
Kermy was playing with his ball. The ball
rolled across the floor. It landed right next
to Pepper's paw.

Pepper sniffed the ball. Then she pushed
the ball with her nose. The ball stopped
right at Kermy's feet.

Kermy looked at Pepper. Then he rolled the ball back.

Pepper got up. She pushed the ball back to Kermy. Kermy rolled the ball to Pepper and Pepper rolled it back. Soon Kermy and Pepper were running all over, chasing each other and pushing the ball.

Kermy and Pepper were not watching where they were going. They were too busy having fun. Suddenly Pepper pushed the ball hard. The little bell inside the ball jingled loudly. It rolled all the way over to where Tabby was napping. The ball bumped right into Tabby's nose!

Tabby had a sleepy look on her face. Then she saw the ball. Kermy and Pepper watched as the look on Tabby's face changed from sleepy to angry. Kermy and Pepper could hear Tabby begin to hiss and growl.

Chapter 4 · Enemies

Pepper barked. Kermy squawked. Just then Max and his mom came home.

"Stop that, cat!" yelled Max. "Go away!"

"I think we should put Tabby out on the porch when we're not home," said Mom.

"That's a good idea," said Dad, who had just come home, too.

Even though Max was waiting for Kermy to talk, he was happy. He loved his pets.

Pepper was happy. When Max was at school she had Kermy to play with. Kermy was happy. He liked to play with Pepper and Max.

The only one who wasn't happy was Tabby. She did not like going outside all day when no people were at home.

Tabby began to watch Kermy very
carefully. If Kermy was playing too close to
Tabby, Tabby started to hiss and growl.
Whenever Pepper heard hissing and
growling, she began to bark. Max would
come running and he always said, "Stop
that, cat! Go away!"

Tabby went away, but she was not
happy. Tabby watched and she waited.

Chapter 5 · No Talking

Days went by, but Kermy did not talk. Kermy sat on Max's finger as Max said, "Hello! Hello!"

Kermy looked at Max. He rubbed his cheek against Max's cheek, but he didn't say a word.

"Mom, Dad," said Max, "I think there's something wrong with Kermy. He won't talk."

"You know, Max, everyone is different. Babies begin to talk at different times. Maybe parrots like Kermy begin to talk at different times, too," Dad said.

Max did not give up. He practiced with Kermy every day. Pepper helped, too. She would bark her hello to Kermy.

Kermy did many funny things. He did some things that were silly and some that were cute. Still Kermy did not talk.

Chapter **6** · All Alone

"Max," said Mom, "are you and Pepper ready to go? Today is the day Pepper goes to the vet for a check-up."

"I think we're all set," said Max. "Be good while we're gone, Kermy."

Kermy played happily with a colored chain. He liked to drag it around as he held it in his beak.

When he got tired of playing with the chain, Kermy went into his cage. He ate a snack of seeds and small pieces of apple. Then he took a drink of water.

Kermy spotted his ball. He hopped to the floor and began to push the ball with his beak.

Tabby watched. This was her chance. She slowly walked up to Kermy. She began to hiss and growl.

Kermy squawked. He fluttered around the floor.

Then Kermy stopped. He looked right at Tabby. He said, "Ruff, ruff! Stop that, cat!"

Tabby stopped right where she was. Who was talking? Who was barking? It sounded just like Max and Pepper.

"Ruff, ruff! Stop that, cat!" said Kermy again. Tabby was confused. She ran away to her bed.

Just then the front door opened. In came Max, Mom, and Pepper. They heard, "Ruff, ruff! Stop that, cat!"

"Oh, no!" said Mom. "We forgot to put Tabby outside before we left!"

"Mom, Mom, come quickly!" said Max. "Kermy is talking! He's really talking!"

"I knew you would talk someday," said Max. "What a smart bird you are!"

Kermy hopped onto Pepper's back. Pepper gave Kermy a ride. Pepper gave a happy bark.

"Ruff, ruff! Stop that, cat! said Kermy.

Glossary

confused   [kun FYOOZD]   mixed up; not understanding

fluttered   [FLUH turd]   flapped quickly, as when moving wings up and down

glum   [glum]   sad, feeling down

idea   [eye DEE uh]   a plan or a picture in the mind

porch   [porch]   a covered way into a building

practiced   [PRAK tust]   did something again and again to learn a skill

squawk   [skwawk]   to make a loud, harsh sound

vet   [vet]   a doctor for animals